Editor's Note

Dear Readers,

I am delighted to present to you our latest issue. In this rapidly evolving world, it is crucial for us to embrace technological advancements ethically and utilize them to propel our purpose forward.

I want to emphasize the importance of pushing through discomfort and not being afraid to move forward. This is especially relevant for men, particularly African American men, as we observe September as Prostate Cancer Awareness Month. It is essential for us to raise awareness about this prevalent disease and encourage early detection and proactive healthcare practices.

Your next level of growth is not only significant for your personal development but also has a profound impact on your family, community, and the world at large. In this issue, we explore areas that continue to push us forward, including technology and storytelling. We firmly believe that sharing our stories can serve as a solution for others who may be facing similar challenges.

Technology has revolutionized the way we live and work, making industries more efficient and accessible than ever before. However, it is crucial to approach these advancements with an ethical mindset. As we embrace the potential of technology, we must also consider its impact on privacy, security, and the overall well-being of individuals and society.

Storytelling, too, has evolved in the digital age. With the rise of social media and online platforms, individuals now have the power to share their stories with a global audience. We delve into the power of storytelling and how it can be used as a means of education, inspiration, and connection. Whether it's through personal essays, memoirs, or fictional narratives, our stories have the potential to create positive change and foster understanding among diverse communities.

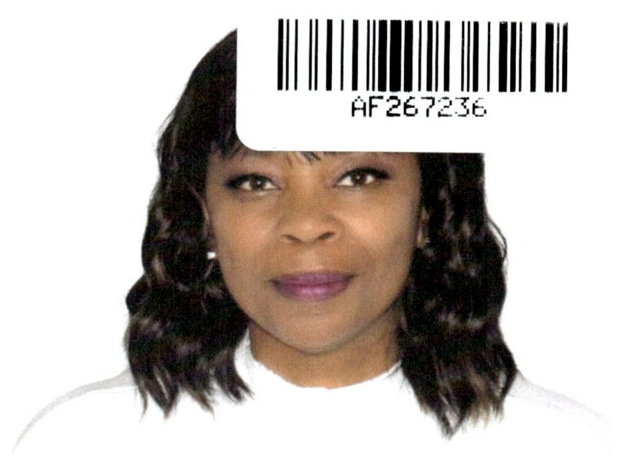

In observance of Prostate Cancer Awareness Month, we shed light on the importance of raising awareness about this disease, particularly among African American men who face higher risks. We aim to provide valuable information and resources that can empower individuals to prioritize their health, seek early detection, and take proactive measures to combat prostate cancer.

As you immerse yourself in the pages of this issue, I encourage you to embrace the possibilities that technology offers. Embrace the discomfort of growth and push through it, knowing that it is essential for your personal and collective development. Share your story, whether it is to enlighten, educate, or entertain, for it has the power to inspire and heal.

Thank you for being a part of our community and for your continued support.

Vikki Jones

Editor-in-Chief

CONTENTS

"Generative AI has triggered a sense of urgency in enterprises worldwide to develop AI strategies. Startups are racing to build disruptive products and business models, while incumbents are looking to respond."

-Jensen Huang

NVIDIA

NVIDIA

Photo Credit: Vikki Jones

NEW
COLLECTION
COMING SOON
VIKKIJONES.COM

SEPTEMBER IS PROSTATE CANCER AWARENESS MONTH: KNOW THE WARNING SIGNS, WHEN TO GET SCREENED

American Cancer Society

Prostate cancer is the second leading cause of cancer death among men in the United States. According to the latest research from scientists at the American Cancer Society (ACS), more than 288,000 men will be diagnosed with the disease this year, with close to 35,000 deaths. Black men are two times more likely to die from the disease than White men and have the highest death rate for prostate cancer of any racial and ethnic group.

Prostate cancer is the second leading cause of cancer death among men in the United States. According to the latest research from scientists at the <u>American Cancer Society</u> (ACS), more than 288,000 men will be diagnosed with the disease this year, with close to 35,000 deaths. Black men are two times more likely to die from the disease than White men and have the highest death rate for prostate cancer of any racial and ethnic group. However, when prostate cancer is detected early, the odds of survival are high. In fact, more than 3.5 million men diagnosed with the disease in the U.S. are still alive today.

Renowned prostate cancer researcher Dr. Lorelei Mucci is the director of strategic research partnerships at the American Cancer Society. Her role includes leading an ACS initiative called <u>IMPACT</u>, or "Improving Mortality Toward Prostate Cancer Together" to address the alarming negative trends in prostate cancer incidence and disparities. For Prostate Cancer Awareness Month Dr. Mucci reviews the signs and symptoms of prostate cancer, including important information about risk factors, PSA screening, and more:

1-Why is it important every September during Prostate Cancer Awarenesss Month to help people learn about the disease?

Despite the alarming statistics concerning the disease, there are opportunities for prevention, early detection, and treatment to improve survival and survivorship and to reduce the burden this cancer has across the U.S. and the globe. Prostate Cancer Awareness Month is so important to have a focused time for men and their families to share knowledge, experiences, and state of science on this important cancer. It is also a time to reflect upon the people who have been impacted by prostate cancer and who have lost their lives to the disease. Also, Prostate Cancer Awareness Month can be an important stimulus to remind public health professionals and government leaders of the need to invest in prevention, early detection, treatment, and improving survivorship.

2- What are the warning signs of prostate cancer?

For some men, prostate cancer may lead to urinary problems, such as having difficulty starting urination or urinating frequently, or pain during ejaculation. This is because of the location of the prostate close to the bladder and urethra. These symptoms and signs also occur with non-cancer conditions, so it is important to follow up with a physician to find out what might be causing these symptoms. If a cancer has already grown beyond the prostate, there may be pain in the hips, back, or other areas that does not go away. For most people, however, there are no signs or symptoms indicating prostate cancer and the cancer is diagnosed with a biopsy following an abnormal blood test.

3- Who is at risk for prostate cancer?

Anyone with a prostate is at risk of prostate cancer, and it is one of the most common cancers. There are some groups that are at higher risk of prostate cancer. For example, our latest research shows Black men and those of African ancestry are 70% more likely to be diagnosed with prostate cancer. Also, the risk of prostate cancer gets higher with age. In addition, people with a family history of prostate cancer (such as in their brother or father) as well as a family history of breast cancer in a sister or mother, are at higher risk of prostate cancer. Part of the family history is due to inherited genetic factors or gene mutations that we now know about. An important note is that while age, family history, and race/ancestry are not modifiable factors (things you can change), there are other factors such as maintaining a healthy body weight, not smoking, and being physically active that can help to offset this higher risk.

4- What is the treatment for prostate cancer? Have there been any advancements in treating the disease?

There are effective treatments for prostate cancer. When the cancer is still confined to the prostate (localized), surgery (radical prostatectomy) and certain forms of radiation are useful to treat and cure prostate cancer. For men who have a low risk of their prostate cancer metastasizing, active surveillance - in which a patient is closely monitored for signs of cancer progression - can also be an important treatment to consider. When the cancer is more aggressive, there are additional therapies that are used, including therapies that target hormonal pathways, chemotherapy, immunotherapy, and radiopharmaceutical therapies. In fact, this is an exciting time in prostate cancer with substantial progress in the discovery and approval of new therapies over the past 5-10 years, as well as several other therapies being developed.

5- Is there a screening test for prostate cancer? Why is it important to catch it early?

Currently, the main screening test for prostate cancer involves taking a blood sample and testing it for the level of a marker called prostate-specific antigen (PSA). Higher levels of PSA in the blood can indicate prostate cancer, but also may be higher in benign conditions such as an enlarged prostate, so it is important to follow up with a doctor to discuss the results and the next steps.

There is good evidence showing that regular PSA screening can reduce prostate cancer mortality, including from randomized trials. However, there is some controversy with screening for prostate cancer since the test can pick up slower-growing cancers that will never lead to harm. An area of active research now is aiming to do more effective screening approaches, targeting the men who are at the highest risk of prostate cancer and then also safely letting people know they can screen less regularly. The ACS launched the "I Love You, Get Screened" campaign to encourage everyone to talk to their loved ones about cancer screening.

6- What age should men be screened for prostate cancer?

The ACS recommends that men at average risk for prostate cancer discuss the benefits and limitations of screening with their healthcare provider at age 50. Men at high risk (which includes Black men in general and any man with a first-degree relative who had prostate cancer before age 65) should have the conversation at age 45. Black men with a family history of breast, ovarian, or prostate cancer, and men with more than one first-degree relative who had prostate cancer at an early age should discuss screening at age 40. Detecting prostate cancer early can lead to more effective treatment and improved outcomes. *For more information on prostate cancer, go to www.cancer.org/cancer/types/prostate-cancer.html.*

TikTok: Empowering Dreams

Written by Vikki Jones

The Most Trendy Fun Ways to Get Your Message Out and Achieve Viral Success

TikTok has taken the world by storm, capturing the attention of millions with its addictive short-form videos. From dance challenges to lip-syncing and DIY hacks, this rapidly growing social media platform has become a hub for creativity and self-expression. However, TikTok isn't just about fun and entertainment; *it has also become a launchpad for individuals to share their messages, grow a global following, and transform their lives.* In this article, we will explore some of the trendiest and most effective ways to use TikTok to get your message out, highlighting success stories of individuals who have gone viral, gained a massive following, and turned their dreams into reality.

1. Engaging Storytelling:
TikTok offers a unique opportunity to captivate audiences through short, visually compelling videos. By harnessing the power of storytelling, individuals can share their experiences, passions, and messages in an engaging way. Whether it's through personal anecdotes, motivational monologues, or relatable content, TikTok users have successfully built a loyal following by connecting with viewers on a deeper level.

2. Educational Content:
TikTok isn't just about entertainment; it also serves as a platform for educating and informing viewers. By creating content that imparts valuable knowledge, individuals can position themselves as experts in their respective fields. Whether it's providing tips and tricks, sharing life hacks, or offering insightful advice, TikTok users have successfully built a dedicated following eager to learn from their expertise.

Success Stories:

TikTok has been a catalyst for numerous success stories, with individuals going from relative obscurity to global fame and fulfilling careers. Take, for example, Charli D'Amelio, who gained a massive following through her captivating dance routines. With over 100 million followers, she has secured brand deals, launched her merchandise, and even starred in music videos, turning her passion for dance into a lucrative profession.

Similarly, Tabitha Brown, a vegan chef, used TikTok to showcase her delicious plant-based recipes and spread positivity. Her infectious personality and cooking skills resonated with millions, leading to a significant increase in her following. Today, she has her own cooking show and has become an influential figure in the vegan community.

TikTok has undoubtedly become a powerful tool for individuals to share their messages, gain global recognition, and turn their dreams into reality. The platform's ability to connect with millions in a short span of time has opened doors for individuals from all walks of life, proving that TikTok is not just a platform for entertainment but a gateway to living one's dreams.

PlayersTV, the premier destination for athlete-driven content, has taken a monumental stride in fan engagement with its groundbreaking Fan Ownership Initiative. This initiative marks a historic moment in sports history, as PlayersTV becomes the world's first athlete fan-owned media company network.

The impressive roster of investor-athletes at PlayersTV reads like a who's who of sports legends. With over 50 NFL, NBA, WNBA, and MLB athletes on board, including Kyrie Irving, Chris Paul, Dwyane Wade, Damian Lillard, Travis Kelce, Vernon Davis, Deandre Jordan, Carmelo Anthony, Natasha Cloud, Angel McCoughtry, AJ Andrews, and many more, PlayersTV has garnered the support of some of the biggest names in the sports world.

These athlete investors not only recognize the significance of this initiative but also endorse its potential to revolutionize the media landscape. Their involvement speaks volumes about the trust and belief they have in PlayersTV's mission to bring athletes and fans closer together.

Deron Guidrey, the visionary founder of PlayersTV, expressed his excitement about the initiative, stating, "Today marks an exciting milestone as we open the doors for fans to become proud owners in PlayersTV, our very own athlete-owned media company. This journey has always been about bringing athletes and fans closer together, and now, by becoming owners, our fans are not just spectators, but integral players in shaping the future and redefining athlete media."

Co-founder Collin Castellaw echoed Guidrey's sentiments, emphasizing that this initiative goes beyond business. "This is more than a business move; it's a movement that celebrates the unity of athletes and fans. We're breaking down barriers and creating an ecosystem where everyone's passion is reflected in every aspect of PlayersTV."

With the Fan Ownership Initiative, PlayersTV is set to redefine the future of sports media. By empowering fans to become shareholders and owners, the network is transforming them from passive viewers into active participants and stakeholders. This move not only strengthens the bond between sports stars and their unwavering supporters but also amplifies the voices of fans and allows them to play a role in shaping the network's future endeavors.

Furthermore, this initiative opens up new avenues for fan engagement and interaction. As stakeholders, fans have the opportunity to provide feedback, suggestions, and ideas for new shows and programming, ensuring that the content reflects their preferences and interests.

PlayersTV's Fan Ownership Initiative is a game-changer in the sports media industry. With the support of an impressive roster of athlete investors, PlayersTV is creating a stronger, more inclusive community and reshaping the future of sports media. This historic move sets a precedent for other networks and demonstrates PlayersTV's commitment to innovation and fan engagement. As the first athlete fan-owned media company, *For more information, visit: www.playerstv.com/invest*.

JONES

WRITTEN BY THE VMH EDITORIAL TEAM

"I believe that every author deserves a chance to share their story, regardless of whether they fit into the traditional publishing mold,".. "I saw a gap in the industry, a need for a platform that could empower authors to bring their stories to life. That's when I decided to create an AI-powered platform that would revolutionize the book publishing process."

PHOTOGRAPHY BY GARRY JONES

In the ever-evolving landscape of publishing and manufacturing, Vikki Jones has emerged as a driving force, revolutionizing the industry with her expertise in AI-powered publishing, global manufacturing, and supply. With her visionary approach, she has created a streamlined process that empowers authors to bring their stories to life with professional high-quality production, author speaker platforms, and media attention/publicity. Vikki Jones has revolutionized the publishing industry with her AI-powered platform by introducing a streamlined process that expedites the publishing journey.

Vikki Jones's passion for books and magazines has always been a driving force in her life. From a young age, she immersed herself in the world of literature, finding solace and inspiration between the pages. Little did she know that her love for reading would one day lead her to become a trailblazer in the publishing industry.

"I always had a deep appreciation for the power of storytelling," Jones reflects. "Books and magazines were my escape, my way of exploring different worlds and perspectives. I never imagined that I would be in this position, leading a company that is revolutionizing the publishing industry. But I am grateful for the opportunity to make a difference and empower authors to share their stories with the world."

Jones's journey took an unexpected turn when she decided to write her own story from a unique perspective, addressing areas of her life that she had never attended to. At the age of 18, she tragically lost her mother to a self-inflicted gunshot wound, leaving her traumatized and in shock. For years, she carried the weight of this experience without healing.

"Writing about that part of my life was a deeper form of self-care for me," Jones reveals. "It allowed me to confront the pain and trauma that I had suppressed for so long. Through my book, I aimed to not only share my story but also inspire others to face their own wounds and embark on a journey of healing."

However, when Jones approached major publishing houses with her manuscript, she faced disappointment. The lack of response or stalling tactics from publishers could have deterred many aspiring authors, but Jones saw it as an opportunity to take matters into her own hands and bridge the gap in the industry.

"I believe that every author deserves a chance to share their story, regardless of whether they fit into the traditional publishing mold," Jones asserts. "I saw a gap in the industry, a need for a platform that could empower authors to bring their stories to life. That's when I decided to create an AI-powered platform that would revolutionize the publishing process."

Through her AI-powered platform, Jones created a streamlined process that expedites the journey from manuscript to publication. This innovative approach not only ensures high-quality production but also empowers authors to take control of their own destiny.

"I wanted to give authors the tools they need to succeed," Jones states. "With my platform, authors no longer have to rely solely on traditional publishing houses. They can now bring their stories to life with professional production and presentation."

"When you publish with us, you maintain full ownership of your work," Jones explains. "We believe that authors should have control over their own creative endeavors and the financial rewards that come with it. That's why we charge an upfront fee to cover our services, but all sales reports and funds deposit directly to you, not to us. We are here to provide the professional literary opportunity you need, not to claim ownership or manage your finances."

By offering authors complete control over their accounts and sales reports, her company - VMH Publishing - ensures transparency and trust in the publishing process. Authors can monitor their book's performance, track their earnings, and make informed decisions about their publishing journey.

"Your story has the power to elevate your life," Jones affirms. "Through your book, you can not only share your message with the world but also create merchandise and additional income streams. We are here to support you every step of the way, providing the tools and resources you need to make the most of your story."

With VMH Publishing, authors can confidently embark on their publishing journey, knowing that their work will be treated with respect and that they will retain full control over their creative endeavors and financial success. Jones's commitment to author empowerment and professional literary opportunities has created a platform where authors can truly thrive, elevating their lives through their stories. But Jones's vision didn't stop at publishing books. She recognized that authors need a platform to showcase their work and engage with readers on a deeper level. This led her to create media and publicity platforms, where authors can connect with their audience and establish themselves as thought leaders.

"Publishing a book is just the beginning of an author's journey," Jones emphasizes. "I wanted to provide authors with a space to share their work, engage with readers, and build a loyal following. Through our communications platforms, authors can showcase their expertise and expand their influence."

Jones's expertise in PR and marketing has also authors, giving them the exposure they need to reach a wider audience.industry connections, I have been able to secure media coverage for authors, helping them reach a wider audience and gain recognition for their work."

Vikki Jones's personal experience of healing through writing has fueled her passion for helping other authors share their stories and find their own paths to healing. Her AI-powered platform not only streamlines the publishing process but also provides a supportive environment for authors to embark on their own journeys of self-discovery.

""I believe that writing has the power to heal and transform lives," Jones affirms. "Through my platform, I want to empower authors to not only share their stories but also find healing and growth in the process. It's about more than just publishing a book; it's about creating a platform for personal transformation."

Jones's platform has already made a significant impact on the publishing industry, with authors from various backgrounds and genres finding success and fulfillment through her streamlined process. The AI-powered platform has not only provided a solution for authors who have struggled to break into the traditional publishing world but has also opened doors for those with unique perspectives and stories that deserve to be heard. *To write your story or to learn more about Vikki Jones visit: vmhpublishing.net or vikkimjones.com for more!*

UNLOCK YOUR LITERARY POTENTIAL WITH VMH PUBLISHING

At VMH Publishing, we stand as a beacon of intellectual excellence, fueling the literary world with our unwavering commitment to literary brilliance. As a distinguished publishing house, we are dedicated to unearthing the limitless potential of language and ushering in a new era of profound literary works.

Whether you're a reader seeking an enthralling narrative, an aspiring author yearning to be discovered, or a literary enthusiast eager to explore new horizons, VMH Publishing invites you to embark on a journey of literary discovery. Immerse yourself in thought-provoking stories, poetic prose, and insightful non-fiction that will leave an indelible mark on your mind and heart.

Visit our website, www.vmhpublishing.net, to explore our captivating catalog and join us in our mission to celebrate the power of words. Together, let's redefine literary excellence and shape the future of literature.

The Future is Here: NVIDIA's Powerful AI Supercomputer and What it Means for Consumers

In a recent announcement, NVIDIA unveiled its amazing new AI supercomputer called the NVIDIA DGX GH200. This supercomputer has the ability to train the next generation of AI models and push the boundaries of technology. Jensen Huang, the CEO of NVIDIA, explains, "With the DGX GH200 AI supercomputer, we are expanding the frontier of AI and enabling digital engines that drive the modern economy."

So, what does this mean for consumers like you and me? Here's what you need to know:

1. Incredible Power: The NVIDIA DGX GH200 is incredibly powerful, capable of performing 1 exaflop of calculations. To put that in perspective, it can process information at a mind-bogglingly fast speed. This power enables researchers and scientists to tackle complex problems and make important breakthroughs.

2. Better AI Models: Thanks to its advanced technology, the DGX GH200 allows for the creation and training of larger AI models. This means that AI systems will become even smarter and more capable. For example, language translation and recommendation systems will improve, making our digital experiences more personalized and efficient.

3. Transforming Industries: The DGX GH200 has the potential to revolutionize various industries such as healthcare, finance, transportation, and entertainment. It opens up new avenues for innovation, enabling organizations to use AI in ways we never thought possible. Imagine better medical diagnoses, more accurate financial predictions, and immersive virtual reality experiences.

4. Efficient Data Processing: The supercomputer's large memory capacity lets it process huge amounts of data quickly and efficiently. This means faster analysis and decision-making based on accurate information. For consumers, it could mean quicker response times from customer service bots or better personalized recommendations when shopping online.

Now, some people worry about the impact of AI on jobs. However, Jensen Huang reassures us, "Everyone becomes a programmer; everyone becomes a creator." What he means is that as AI evolves, it

opens up new opportunities for people to learn and adapt. While some jobs may be automated, new roles will emerge that require human creativity and expertise. NVIDIA's DGX GH200 represents a significant step forward in AI technology. It not only pushes the boundaries of what's possible but also presents exciting possibilities for consumers. This supercomputer has the potential to transform industries, improve AI models, and process data more efficiently. While concerns about job displacement exist, it's essential to recognize that AI also brings opportunities for innovation and learning. As we move into the future, the potential for everyone to become a programmer and creator becomes more attainable.

The future is here with NVIDIA's powerful AI supercomputer. With its immense capabilities and advancements, it has the potential to reshape the way we live, work, and interact with technology. So get ready for a future where AI becomes even more intelligent and where you might just find yourself becoming a programmer and creating amazing things.

What is
THE
SIMPLICITY OF
INDULGING
ONES PASSION

Ignite Passion for Your Work and Thrive

Passion Stimulates Value & Success If you have dreams, goals, and aspirational things you want to do with your life, go for it! Associate with people who will add to you and your goals versus take away from them. Get away from those folks that don't support your idea, and surround yourself with people that support and value you - help you grow.

@vmhmagazine

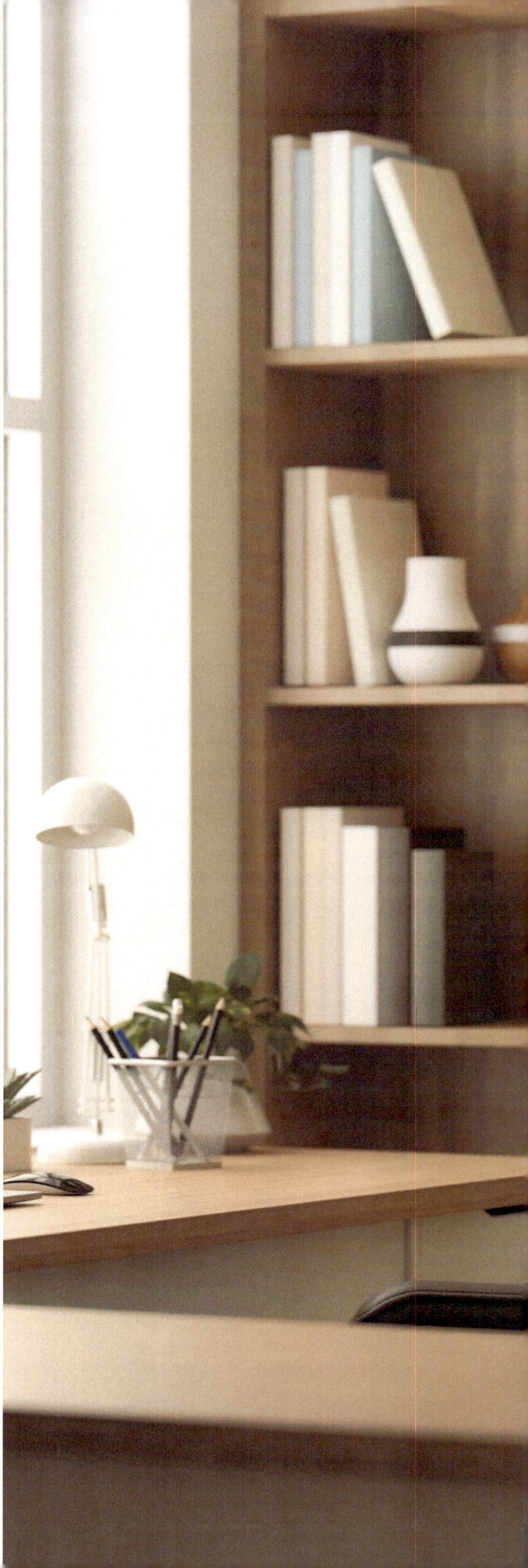

TRAVEL

WHERE YOUR JOURNEY BEGINS

@shopvikkijones

Featured speakers in Dubai include:

- **H.E Thani Al Zeyoudi,** minister of state for foreign trade, **UAE**

- **Bertrand Conqueret,** president global supply chain company and corporate senior vice president purchasing, **Henkel**

- **Mourad Tamoud,** executive vice-president, global supply chain, **Schneider Electric**

- **Sujay Sarkar,** senior vice-president and group head corporate finance, **Olam Agri**

- **Mayra Souza,** global trade director, **International Flavors & Fragrances**

- **Assel Zhanassova,** CEO, Kazpost, former vice-minister of trade and integration, **Republic of Kazakhstan**

- **Ralph Ossa,** chief economist, **WTO**

- **Lisa Schroeter,** global director of trade and investment policy, **Dow**

- **Adam Kaminski,** chief supply chain officer, **Aujan Group**

- **Leila Afas,** director, global public policy, **Toyota**

Sponsors

Official host

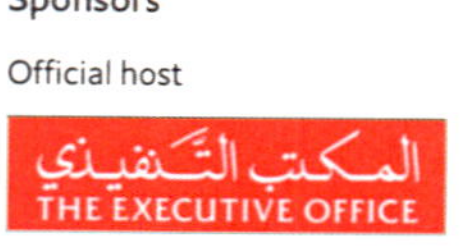

Lead sponsor

J.P.Morgan

Platinum sponsor

Media partners

www.events.economist.com/global-trade-week

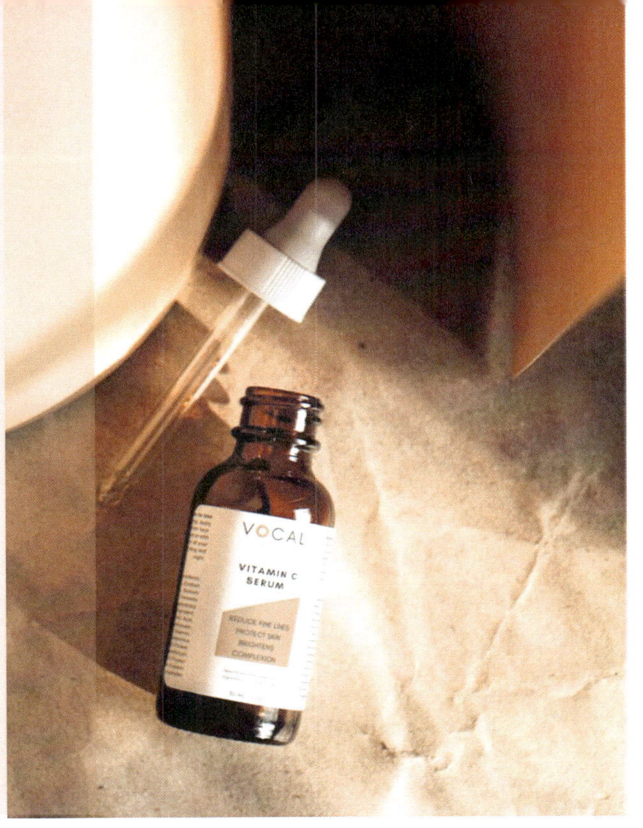

NOURISH
HYDRATE
YOUR SKIN

EXCELLENT
SKIN CARE
FOR ALL
SKIN
TONES!

More info: www.vocalskincare.com

PROMOTING EMOTIONAL WELL-BEING THROUGH RABBIT-ASSISTED THERAPY

"The effect of rabbit-assisted interventions on the anxiety levels of first-grade children at a primary school was analyzed…Rabbit-assisted interventions proved to be efficient, as anxiety level scores were significantly lower during the animal-assisted periods."

- NIH (National Institute of Health)

Services offered by The Painted Bunny:

- Rabbit-Assisted Therapy Sessions
- Classroom Interventions for Emotional Well-being
- Fun Activities for Children:
  - Face Painting
  - Balloon Twisting
-Time with a Painted Live Bunny & More

GET IN TOUCH FOR NATIONWIDE CUSTOM SOLUTIONS

Contact Us Today at:

www.thepaintedbunny.com

SIGGRAPH 2023: Celebrating 50 Years of *Breakthroughs and Innovation in Computer Graphics and Interactive Techniques*

SIGGRAPH 2023, the premier conference and exhibition on computer graphics and interactive techniques, recently celebrated its 50th year with a week-long extravaganza in the vibrant city of Los Angeles. This milestone event brought together industry professionals, pioneers, students, artists, and technicians from around the world to commemorate the remarkable advancements and achievements in the field over the past five decades. What began as a humble ACM SIGGRAPH History archive grew into an extraordinary project that involved over 225 individuals collaborating globally. The aim was not only to celebrate the past but also to embrace the present and future of computer graphics. The historical offerings at SIGGRAPH 2023 ranged from Retrospective Talks, which delved into pivotal moments in the industry's evolution, to an immersive journey through the early hardware developments in the interactive Time Tunnel, sponsored by Autodesk. This impressive installation showcased the most comprehensive timeline of computer graphics achievements from the last 50 years.

One individual who has dedicated his career to exploring the intersection of technology and creativity is Hiroaki Kitano, the Senior Executive Vice President and Chief Technology Officer of Sony Group Corporation. As a keynote speaker at SIGGRAPH 2023, sponsored by Sony, Kitano will delve into the impact of technology on the creative process. He will share remarkable stories of creators within the Sony Group who have harnessed the power of both creativity and technology to bring their visions to life. Kitano's insights will shed light on the transformative potential of bridging these two domains.

SIGGRAPH 2023 stands as a testament to the continuous growth and innovation within the computer graphics and interactive techniques industry. It serves as a platform for professionals and enthusiasts to come together, exchange ideas, and push the boundaries of what is possible. With each passing year, the conference showcases the latest advancements, trends, and breakthroughs in the field, inspiring a new generation of artists, researchers, and technologists.

The SIGGRAPH 50th celebration brought together innovators, researchers, and creators of digital art, visual effects, artificial intelligence, virtual reality, and much more. The contributions came from a variety of fields — including arts, science and electronics, academia and research, film, and television, among others. The work shown at the SIGGRAPH conference comes from diverse industries and government agencies, from medical, scientific visualization, artificial life, and robotics to games and animation in the entertainment field.

"SIGGRAPH looks forward to daring and bold ideas, research, and advancements coming from the community, but we also benefit from looking back at the contributions made by the community that got us to where we are today," said Erik Brunvand, SIGGRAPH 2023 Conference Chair. "It's young enough of a discipline that many of the pioneers are still able to celebrate with us. We have a rich history where our early innovators created incredibly creative concepts that are still making an impact today."—

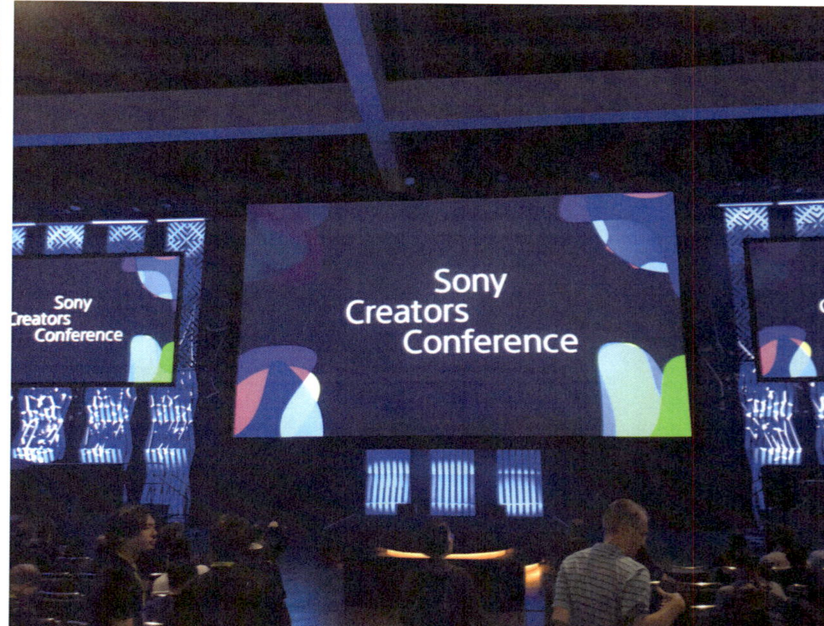

PERSONAL GROWTH & SUCCESS
UNLOCKING YOUR GREATEST POTENTIAL

Life is a journey of constant growth and self-discovery. Often, we find ourselves in a state of complacency, unaware that there is a greater place waiting for us. It is during these uncomfortable moments that we have the opportunity to develop our character, enhance our skills, and prepare ourselves for the next level. Embracing discomfort becomes the key to unlocking our greatest potential. In this editorial, we will explore the importance of pushing through, focusing, and challenging ourselves to reach new heights in life.

1. The Comfort Zone Illusion:

The comfort zone is a deceptive place, where we may feel safe and secure, but it hinders our personal growth. It is in the discomfort that we truly learn and evolve as individuals. Stepping out of our comfort zone allows us to expand our horizons, face new challenges, and discover hidden talents. Embracing discomfort is the first step towards breaking free from the limitations we set for ourselves.

2. Character Development:

When faced with discomfort, we are forced to confront our fears and insecurities. This process builds resilience, determination, and character. Overcoming obstacles strengthens our mental and emotional muscles, enabling us to handle future challenges with greater ease. Embracing discomfort becomes an opportunity for personal growth and self-improvement, shaping us into stronger and more capable individuals.

3. Skill Enhancement:

In the pursuit of our greatest place, we must continuously refine and develop our skills. Embracing discomfort pushes us to acquire new knowledge, learn from our mistakes, and adapt to unfamiliar situations. It is through these experiences that we acquire the expertise and abilities necessary to excel in our chosen fields. Each moment of discomfort becomes an opportunity to sharpen our skills and become better versions of ourselves.

4. Preparation for the Next Level:

Life is a series of stepping stones, and each discomfort we encounter prepares us for the next level. By embracing discomfort, we become better equipped to handle the challenges that lie ahead. Our ability to adapt, persevere, and thrive in uncomfortable situations becomes a valuable asset as we progress towards our goals.

Embracing discomfort is not only about reaching our greatest place but also about preparing ourselves for the journey that follows.

5. Determination and Intentionality:

To embrace discomfort, we must approach it with determination and intentionality. It is not enough to simply endure discomfort; we must actively seek out opportunities for growth and self-improvement. This requires setting clear goals, breaking them down into manageable steps, and committing ourselves to the process.

With a focused mindset and unwavering determination, we can navigate through discomfort and emerge stronger on the other side.

Embracing discomfort is a necessary step in our journey towards self-actualization. It is through these uncomfortable moments that we learn, grow, and prepare ourselves for our greatest place in life. By stepping out of our comfort zone, we develop our character, enhance our skills, and become better equipped to face the challenges that lie ahead. Let us embrace discomfort with determination and intentionality, knowing that our greatest potential awaits us on the other side.

COMFORTABLE CARRYING OPTIONS

Say goodbye to uncomfortable bags. Vikki Jones' designs prioritize comfort, with padded straps, ergonomic handles, and lightweight construction, ensuring a comfortable carrying experience even during long journeys.

Need extra space? Jones' bags feature expandable compartments, allowing you to increase the capacity when needed. Travel with confidence, knowing you have room for souvenirs or extra work documents.

Updating your home can provide the perfect opportunity to explore new design styles or refresh living spaces with a new color scheme. In fact, a coat of paint can help set the mood for entire rooms in your home.

By turning to nature-inspired designs, you can create a sense of comfort and relaxation. A hybrid color, like Valspar's 2024 Color of the Year, Renew Blue, is gentle and airy with a touch of blue to set a restful and meditative mood. The grayed sea green – inspired by fleeting things such as fog, mist, clouds and glacier lakes – is a seasonless and versatile hue that features a mid-tone blue with warm undertones and can be used in outdoor living spaces and four-season rooms alike.

"This mid-tone shade has become popular for wellness environments over the years due to its low saturation level, which evokes a sense of rest and calm," said Sue Kim, Valspar's director of color marketing. "The harmonious green and blue open the possibility for outdoor applications, blurring the boundary between interior and exterior."

To help elevate the mood in your home, consider implementing Renew Blue into one of these popular design trends that can update the look of nearly any of your indoor or outdoor spaces.

Coastal
Coastal looks are timeless designs that have remained relevant for years because of their positive correlation to calming beach locations. Perfect for outdoor spaces like the backyard, you can implement a more curated and personal take on the trend by shifting from "typical" coastal design that pairs beachy hues with natural textures like rope, driftwood and wicker to something more classic and natural like the Cape Cod variation by working in some nautical touches like anchors, oars or seashells.

Modern Farmhouse
In the entryway, using beautiful and functional decor, such as unique ceramics and handwoven textiles, helps usher in a modern rustic style. By using timeless tones and accents, as well as layering heritage art, you can create visual mystery while elevating the ordinary to make your home feel warm and welcoming to guests from the moment they walk through the door.

Nordic Comfort
Modern Traditional is a style that came together over time and the Hygge look is a refined take. It pulls elementary cues from traditional farmhouse style but has shaker-inspired elements mixed in and is done with a slightly modern twist. It can make a larger space like the kitchen feel welcoming, open, carefully curated and warm.

Modern Boho
Boho is a nature-loving and free-spirited style connected to earthy and botanical elements. From handmade decor to vintage

metallic finishes, this style reimagines the past and elevates everyday spaces like bathrooms into personal retreats designed with wellness in mind.

Pastel Wabi-Sabi
Leaning into the modern sentiment of "less is more," this style reflects a naturally minimalist design aesthetic and showcases color coordination with mood-boosting hues and joyful color. Perfect for nurseries and other spaces that should be bright and welcoming, pieces with pared-back, welcoming shapes and silhouettes that allow quality natural materials to shine are perfect for decorating the room.

Visit Valspar.com to find more on-trend home design inspiration and order up to 10 free paint chips to be delivered to your home to see how your favorite colors will fit your space.

Mastering the Mindset: Letting Go with Confidence

Written by Vikki Jones

Those who possess a mindset that understands the power of doing what they can and trusting that the rest will fall into place, open doors to a life filled with joy, productivity, and abundance. This transformative mindset allows individuals to advance in less time, realizing that what is meant for them will come their way, and nothing can impede their journey towards greatness.

The key to unlocking this powerful mindset lies in adopting an unwavering belief that each of us holds the capacity to produce our best work, be the best version of ourselves, and continuously strive for personal growth. It is this unwavering commitment to self-improvement that propels individuals towards their goals, enabling them to surpass limitations and achieve remarkable success.

By embracing this positive mindset, we tap into a wellspring of joy that fuels our actions and fuels our productivity. When we approach tasks with a sense of purpose and enthusiasm, we not only enjoy what we do, but we also find that we accomplish more in less time. This is because joy and productivity go hand in hand - when we are genuinely passionate about our work, we become more focused, creative, and efficient. As a result, we are able to achieve our goals faster and with greater ease.

Furthermore, this mindset attracts abundance into our lives. When we align our thoughts and actions with positivity and gratitude, we open ourselves up to a world of limitless possibilities. It is through this mindset that we attract opportunities, connections, and resources that contribute to our personal and professional growth.

However, it is crucial to remember that this mindset does not guarantee a life free from challenges or setbacks. Instead, it equips us with the resilience and determination to overcome obstacles and learn from failures. By focusing on our own growth and development, we become better equipped to navigate through life's inevitable hurdles, emerging stronger and more resilient with each experience.

In conclusion, adopting a mindset that understands the power of doing what we can and trusting that the rest will fall into place is a transformative approach to life. It brings forth joy, productivity, and abundance, allowing us to advance in less time. By acknowledging that what is meant for us will come our way, we can focus on producing our best work, being the best versions of ourselves, and continuously striving for personal growth. So, let us embrace this mindset and unlock our boundless potential, for it is within us to create a life filled with success, fulfillment, and happiness.

JUNIPER
GLOBAL

Connecting people with
their style.

Procurement
Manufacturing
Supply

⊕ juniperglobalvision.com

BOOSTING SMALL AND MEDIUM-SIZED BUSINESSES:

HOW AI AND CHATGPT CAN HELP

Written by Vikki Jones

Have you ever wondered how big companies always seem to have the upper hand when it comes to new technologies like Artificial Intelligence (AI)? It's because they have the money and staff to quickly jump on the AI bandwagon and make the most of it, while small and medium-sized businesses (SMEs) struggle to keep up. But shouldn't there be a way for smaller companies to increase their profits and tap into the full potential of AI too?

Well, the good news is that there is hope for SMEs to level the playing field and benefit from AI and the recently released ChatGPT. These fancy tech tools have a lot to offer, but it's understandable that smaller businesses might be hesitant to trust and adopt them. After all, they don't have an army of tech experts at their disposal like the big guys do.

But fear not, because there are practical ways for SMEs to embrace AI and ChatGPT without breaking the bank or feeling overwhelmed. The first step is education and awareness. SMEs need to take the time to learn about the benefits and possibilities that AI and ChatGPT can bring to their operations.

By understanding how these technologies can improve efficiency and productivity in specific areas, SMEs can start reaping the rewards.

Building trust is another crucial factor. AI might seem like a scary and unpredictable thing, but SMEs can ease their worries by partnering with reliable AI providers and starting with small-scale pilot projects. Seeing tangible results and success stories within their own industry will help SMEs gain confidence in AI as a valuable tool for their business.

Collaboration is key too. SMEs can team up with other small businesses or even larger companies to share resources, expertise, and navigate the AI landscape together. By working together, they can overcome the lack of technical talent and benefit from collective knowledge, which will ultimately level the playing field against their bigger competitors.

It's also important for governments and industry associations to lend a helping hand. They can offer incentives, grants, and specialized programs to support SMEs in implementing AI technologies. By creating an environment that promotes knowledge-sharing, collaboration, and innovation, policymakers can empower SMEs to fully embrace AI and unlock its potential.

Yes, the challenges of adopting AI and ChatGPT might seem challenging for SMEs, but it's important to remember that every new technology brings opportunities for growth and success. By seeking knowledge, building trust, embracing collaboration, and taking advantage of supportive policies, small and medium-sized businesses can harness the power of AI and ChatGPT to increase their profits, work more efficiently, and thrive in a competitive market.

PRACTICAL WAYS
SME'S CAN UTILIZE AI

Small and medium-sized enterprises (SMEs) can leverage the power of Artificial Intelligence (AI) in various ways to enhance their operations, improve efficiency, and drive growth.

1. **Customer Service and Support:** AI-powered chatbots and virtual assistants can handle customer inquiries, provide real-time support, and offer personalized recommendations. These AI-driven solutions can streamline customer interactions, reduce response times, and improve customer satisfaction, even outside regular business hours.

2. **Data Analysis and Insights:** AI algorithms can process large volumes of data quickly and accurately, enabling SMEs to gain valuable insights. By analyzing customer behavior, market trends, and operational data, SMEs can make informed decisions, identify patterns, and predict future trends. This helps in optimizing marketing strategies, inventory management, and overall business operations.

3. **Predictive Maintenance:** AI can help SMEs implement predictive maintenance strategies by analyzing data from sensors and machines. By detecting patterns and anomalies, AI algorithms can predict equipment failures or maintenance needs, allowing SMEs to proactively address issues before they escalate. This minimizes downtime, reduces maintenance costs, and extends the lifespan of machinery and assets.

4. **Process Automation:** AI-powered automation can streamline repetitive and time-consuming tasks, freeing up employees to focus on more strategic and value-added activities. SMEs can use AI to automate data entry, invoice processing, inventory management, and other routine tasks, improving operational efficiency and reducing errors.

5. **Sales and Marketing Optimization:** AI can enhance SMEs' sales and marketing efforts by analyzing customer data, identifying leads, and personalizing marketing campaigns. AI algorithms can segment customers based on their preferences, purchase history, and behavior, enabling SMEs to deliver targeted and relevant marketing messages. This helps in boosting conversion rates, increasing customer engagement, and optimizing sales funnels.

6. **Personalized Customer Experiences:** AI enables SMEs to deliver personalized experiences by analyzing customer preferences, behavior, and past interactions. AI algorithms can recommend products, content, and services tailored to each customer's specific needs and interests. This enhances customer satisfaction, loyalty, and drives repeat business.

7. **Market Research and Competitive Analysis:** SMEs can leverage AI to gather and analyze market data, customer reviews, social media sentiment, and competitor information. AI-powered tools can provide valuable insights into market trends, consumer preferences, and competitive intelligence. This helps SMEs make data-driven decisions, identify market gaps, and develop competitive strategies.

8. **Virtual Collaboration and Communication:** With the rise of remote work, AI-powered virtual collaboration tools can facilitate communication, project management, and knowledge sharing among remote teams. AI-driven solutions can automate scheduling, generate meeting summaries, and provide real-time language translation, enabling SMEs to collaborate effectively across borders and time zones.

Black-Owned Business Support

American Express is committed to providing access to capital and financial education to at least **250,000 Black-owned small and medium-sized businesses** in the U.S. by 2024, as part of its $1 billion action plan to enhance diverse representation and promote equal opportunities for colleagues, customers and communities.

Our Approach to Empowering Black-owned Businesses:

Driving Sales & Growth

Marketing support and access to contracts, all to help Black-owned businesses reach more customers and unlock more business opportunities

Offering Funding

Funding options, such as grants and loans, to jump start and grow Black-owned businesses

Providing Tools & Resources

Education, resources and tools to help Black-owned businesses manage and grow their businesses with confidence

Driving Sales & Growth

ByBlack

American Express and the U.S. Black Chambers, Inc. are expanding ByBlack with the launch of the first national certification program exclusively for Black-ownership designation. First created as a directory of Black-owned businesses, the no-cost, digital platform now unlocks more ways for Black-owned businesses across the country to reach new customers and secure contracting opportunities. ByBlack provides businesses with an approved accreditation trusted by customers and enables consumers and companies to easily find Black-owned businesses to buy from. American Express also plans to increase spend with Black-owned suppliers to at least $100 million annually by 2024.

Contract Connections

American Express continues to support small and mid-size businesses through Contract Connections – a long-standing series that connects Black-owned suppliers with large corporate and government buyers to discuss business opportunities in one-on-one meetings.

Signage and Supplies

Last summer, American Express launched new marketing materials for Amex-welcoming businesses to use to attract Card Members wanting to spend at Black-owned establishments. Items include branded window decals, point of purchase stickers, and digital image files to place on company's website.

Offering Funding

Accion Opportunity Fund

American Express partnered with Accion Opportunity Fund, a leading non-profit small business lender, on a new program to provide loans and other resources to underfunded small business owners in the U.S., including people of color, women and immigrants. American Express is providing $40M to Accion Opportunity Fund, the largest investment the nonprofit has received since its founding.

Coalition to Back Black Business

American Express established the Coalition to Back Black Businesses, a first-of-its-kind collaboration with the U.S. Chamber of Commerce Foundation and four major Black chambers, including the National Black Chamber of Commerce, the National Business League, the U.S. Black Chambers, Inc., and Walker's Legacy. The Coalition provides grants to Black-owned businesses to support their long-term resilience. The company made a $10 million commitment to fund the grant program and support Black-owned small business recovery in the U.S. over the next four years.

100 for 100

Together with IFundWomen of Color, American Express launched the 100 for 100 program, surprising 100 Black women entrepreneurs with grants of $25,000 each and access to 100 days of business resources — including business education, mentorship, marketing, virtual networking and more — to help them jumpstart their ventures.

Backing Historic Small Restaurants

American Express, in partnership with the National Trust for Historic Preservation, launched "Backing Historic Small Restaurants," a more than $1 million investment to preserve historic restaurants in the U.S. as they continue to navigate the pandemic and plan for recovery. 25 historic and culturally significant restaurants across the U.S. owned by underrepresented groups have received funding and resources.

Providing Tools & Resources

Business Class is a suite of educational and entertaining business resources, in the form of content and events, all available at no cost. American Express has created hundreds of resources for the small business community under the Business Class umbrella, including articles on the Business Trends & Insights website, Daily Edit e-newsletters and "Office Hours" on Instagram Live where followers hear from well-known entrepreneurs.

The Home Depot Foundation Invests $6 Million in Skilled Trades Training - New Scholarship and Entrepreneurship Partnerships

The Home Depot Foundation announced an incremental investment of more than $6 millionin skilled trades training and launched new strategic partnerships to address the nearly 400,000 job openings across the construction industry. With these philanthropic grants, the *Foundation's Path to Pro program* launched a brand new entrepreneurship program and will provide free, skilled trades training and scholarships for more veterans, military families, high school students and separating service members.

To serve aspiring entrepreneurs within the skilled trades industry, The Home Depot Foundation is partnering with Bunker Labs to introduce an entrepreneurship program designed to guide U.S. military veterans and military spouses through the process of establishing a successful business foundation. During the 8-week program, participants will gain industry-specific mentorship, learn about market segmentation, how to address specific customer profiles and design a business plan for launch. The program's virtual offering makes it accessible to participants nationwide.

The Foundation is also expanding its Path to Pro scholarship program with grants to SkillPointe Foundation, its partner since 2021, and through a new partnership with Folds of Honor. Military scholarships through Folds of Honor extend financial support to qualifying veterans and military family members entering or enrolled in accredited skilled trade schools.

"We're expanding our current training programs and creating new avenues to steadily fill the country's skilled labor gap with in-demand talent," said The Home Depot Foundation's executive director, Shannon Gerber. "Diversifying our approach with additional entrepreneurship and scholarship programs helps ensure we're reaching more communities with free training opportunities and creating sustainable change for the industry."

The Home Depot Foundation extended its grant to long-time partner Home Builders Institute to broaden its Path to Pro high school and military programs. The two organizations will continue to provide no-cost PACT curriculum certification for more than 1,200 separating military members annually, 11th and 12th grade students and Title 1 schools nationwide.

The Home Depot Foundation's skilled trades training program, Path to Pro, launched in 2018 with a $50 million commitment to train the next generation of skilled tradespeople, diversify the trades industry, and address the growing labor shortage in the U.S. The Foundation's trades-focused partnerships have introduced more than 200,000 people to the skilled trades and have trained more than 41,000 participants through programming available to youth, high school students, underserved communities and separating U.S. military.

Beyond the Foundation's work in this area, The Home Depot's Path to Pro Network connects skilled tradespeople to professional contractors and job openings. *For more information and to find skilled trades resources available in English and Spanish, visit PathtoPro.com.*

PathtoPro.com
One stop shop for trades prospects, parents, and influencers

Youth Programs *
- Curriculum, hands-on training for entry-level trades prospects
- Construction Ready and Home Builders Institute programs (270 schools)
Made possible by The Home Depot Foundation

Connect to Pros for Hire

Path to Pro Network
- Free network where trade professionals are hiring skilled workers
- Thousands of available trade jobs nationwide
- Millions of hiring Pros can create job postings and search skilled candidates through the Pro Xtra Loyalty program

THE BOOKSHELF

VMH PUBLISHING

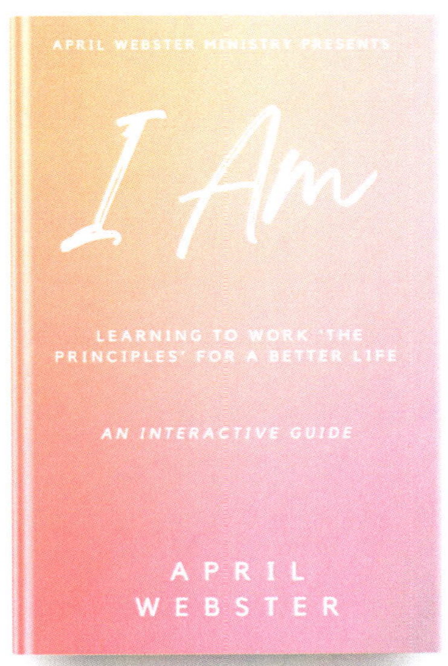

I AM - Learning To Work 'The Principles' For a Better Life

In this book, Dr. April Webster explores twelve affirmations to declare inward strength to her readers. I AM is a metaphysical name of the spiritual self. It is the presence of God with in you. When the words I AM are spoken it is a declaration. I AM is the mere fact of our existence and once you become aware of it you hold the power in your words. Dr. Webster has personally discovered the power of spoken words. This is not a book to be read only once then put away on a book shelf or in a storage bin. This book is intended to be read and repeated over and over until one becomes fully aware of who they really are called to be. This book requires the readers to take action.
.

By following these principles, you hold the power of transforming your life to another level beyond your current position. Dr. Webster provides the steps needed to act and apply these principles to your life. You will walk and operate in another dimension once you become aware of who you really are.

Prioritize Self-Care Guide & Workbook

Self-care is any activity which helps you to enhance your well-being and maintain your health - both physical and mental. This means self-care can be anything from eating nourishing food or getting enough sleep, to setting aside time for a creative or spiritual endeavor. Prioritizing self makes us happier, healthier, better people - so why do we so often struggle to actually put it into practice?

However, prioritizing yourself can make you feel more empowered, more secure, and more content with your everyday life. Even choices that seem difficult, such as setting tough boundaries or asking your family members to help you out around the house, can have long-term benefits that help you feel loved and ultimately strengthen your connections to those in your life.

My Best Kept Secret Memoir

"My Best Kept Secret Memoir" is a powerful and inspiring collection of personal stories shared by the author, aimed at empowering women who have endured incidents of abuse. Through her heartfelt narratives, she aims to encourage healing, resilience, and the strength to break free from the shackles of abuse. This memoir is an essential read for anyone seeking to reclaim their lives.

Is It Really All About Our Young Football Players

We repeatedly hear that it's really all about our young football players, but is it really? You decide. After reading this book, you'll have a better understanding of America's most popular sport - football. As well as how our young football players have a major role in football.

JASMINE TOOKES JOINS ANNE KLEIN TO COMMEMORATE THE BATTLE OF VERSAILLES ANNIVERSARY

Written by Vikki Jones | Photos Courtesy: Atelier PR

In a powerful collaboration that celebrates both fashion history and female empowerment, supermodel and entrepreneur Jasmine Tookes has joined forces with iconic American brand Anne Klein. Together, they are set to commemorate the 50th anniversary of the historic Battle of Versailles, a turning point for American sportswear in the global fashion scene.

Anne Klein, a brand synonymous with timeless style, is marking this significant year with the release of their Fall/Winter 2023 fashion campaign. Featuring Jasmine Tookes as the face of the campaign, the collection captures the essence of a modern woman navigating a fast-paced world with grace and confidence. With this partnership, Anne Klein and Jasmine Tookes pay homage to the brand's legacy and the everlasting impact of the Battle of Versailles.

Photographed on the bustling streets of New York City by the renowned Tom Schirmacher, the Anne Klein Fall/Winter '23 campaign brings to life a collection of rich classics, perfectly suited for any occasion. Jasmine Tookes effortlessly showcases these designs, adding her own touch of elegance and personality to each look.

The Battle of Versailles, an event that revolutionized global fashion and propelled American sportswear to the forefront, holds deep significance for Anne Klein. To honor this pivotal moment, Anne Klein will collaborate with NYFW: The Talks to host a panel discussion titled "Battle of Versailles 50: The Making of Fashion History." Moderated by Jasmine Tookes herself, the panel will feature esteemed guests including designer Stephen Burrows, the last surviving designer from

the original ten, Donna Karan, Anne Klein's right hand during that time, and trailblazing models Alva Chinn and Pat Cleveland, whose unforgettable catwalk styles forever changed the industry. Jameel Spencer, CMO in Residence for Anne Klein, speaks proudly about the brand's legacy, stating, "We take immense pride in honoring Anne's legacy and keeping that flame alive. The Battle of Versailles not only showcased Anne Klein's work on a global stage, but it also sparked social change, racial awareness, and American magic. As we celebrate multiple milestones this year, including what would have been our founder's 100th birthday, we are thrilled to partner with Jasmine Tookes to recognize the strength of diverse women impacting the world positively, all while exuding style and grace."

Jasmine Tookes, shared her enthusiasm for the collaboration, saying, "*I am thrilled to be a small part of this storied brand founded by a powerful woman. My power as a woman lies in my positivity and being able to serve as a role model for mothers and businesswomen, gracefully managing it all with style.*"

This collaboration between Jasmine Tookes and Anne Klein not only pays tribute to the past but also paves the way for a future where diverse women continue to inspire and empower individuals worldwide. Together, they showcase the timeless appeal of wardrobe choices that transcend trends and exude a sense of confidence and individuality. *For more information on Jasmine, visit www.thelionsmanagement.com, or @TheLionsMgmt on Instagram.*

ANNE KLEIN

5 Tips to Manage Money Smarter

There's more to managing your money than paying your bills and successfully avoiding overdraft charges (although those are definitely steps in the right direction). Effectively managing your money takes time and planning, but the payoff may be a stronger financial future.

Create a budget. Some people avoid making a monthly budget because they think they don't need one. However, having a clear idea of the money coming in and going out of your bank account each month can help you make better spending decisions. A budget doesn't have to be complicated; it can be as simple as a spreadsheet that lists your monthly income and expenses. Be sure to consider long-term debt, like student loans, and treat your savings account as a payee you owe each month.

Track your spending. In a similar vein, it's a good idea to see where your non-bill-related spending goes. For example, you may stop by the grocery store more frequently than you realize, and each of those trips is likely going to cost you more than if you limited it to just once or twice a week. Many banks and credit institutions offer charts and graphs that break down your spending so you can see exactly where your money is going and use that information to make adjustments.

Research big purchases. What constitutes "big" may vary depending on your circumstances and financial status, but regardless of the dollar amount, doing some due diligence before purchases is a good idea. The average millennial will do 4.6 hours of research before buying a big-ticket item like a mattress or car, according to a survey conducted by OnePoll on behalf of Mattress Firm.

Millennials are also likely to seek input from others, with one in five consulting four or more people for their opinions on a purchase.

"Doing research before making a big purchase can make all the difference," said Timothy Mayes, Mattress Firm's senior manager of eCommerce merchandising. "There are several resources available such as online reviews, blogs and even guides on the best time to buy that can help save you money on larger purchases. If you find yourself overwhelmed with too many options, recommendations from friends and family are the best resources to help you narrow down your choices."

Prepare for emergencies. If a single unexpected event would cripple you financially, it's a good idea to build an emergency fund that could help you weather through a storm. A job loss, accident or illness would substantially alter your income, expenses or both, so having at least a few months of salary stashed in savings could make a major difference in how long that unfortunate scenario affects your life.

Finance purchases responsibly. Building credit takes time and responsibility, but if you don't ever borrow money, you won't have a chance to earn the rates reserved for exceptional credit holders. Financing a moderately sized purchase, such as a mattress, is a good starting point. It may be out of reach for a cash payment, but the balance you carry could be paid in a reasonably short timeframe. To build good credit, always make payments on time and make monthly payments larger than the minimum payment – which is usually just the interest – so you're actually paying down the principal. Following these tips and taking advantage of product sites that offer resources and information on a potential purchase may aid in your long-term financial health. Find more information at MattressFirm.com/blog.

Work-life Balance

Unwind, Recharge, Succeed

Finding the right balance between work and personal life can feel like an elusive goal. Introducing our new 'Unatosha' work-life balance candle, designed to help you create a harmonious environment that fosters productivity, relaxation, and personal growth.

A4J Luxury Sports Line
Coming Soon